Christian Festivals

Reclaiming a Biblical Theology

Mark Fraser

Assistant Curate at St Paul's, Astley Bridge, Bolton

GROVE BOOKS LIMITED

RIDLEY HALL RD CAMBRIDGE CB3 9HU

Contents

The Cover Illustration is by Peter Ashton

First Impression January 2006
ISSN 1470-8531
ISBN 1 85174 612 9

1 Introduction

Between the months of April and October 2006 over 200,000 people will attend a Christian 'festival' somewhere in Britain.

By this I do not, of course, mean Easter or Pentecost in a church but rather any of over 30 gatherings which will take place across the length and breadth of the country—from the CLAN gathering in St Andrews, Scotland to Detling Bible Week in Kent, from Spring Harvest in Skegness to Summer Madness in Belfast. These events are very diverse and it is possible that their organizing bodies would be surprised, and perhaps perturbed, to be grouped together under the banner of 'festivals.' However, in recent times 'festival' has mutated into a popular and generic term for events advertising themselves under a variety of labels. These include the 'traditional' Bible week, all manner of conferences and even holidays in addition to what might more traditionally be understood as festival.

The word 'festival' derives from the Latin for feast and implies aspects of joyous celebration, expressions of cultural identity through music and drama, and regular annual observance. Our events satisfy these criteria and offer annual banquets of biblical exposition, smorgasbords of worship experience and feasts of fellowship opportunities. Such festivals are a significant part of the life of the modern church, and as such raise a number of questions which we do well to consider as we pray and work for the coming of the kingdom.

Such festivals raise a number of questions which we do well to consider as we pray and work for the coming of the Kingdom

Moreover, this 'festival' scene is expanding rapidly with attendances rising and the number of events proliferating. The Christian arts festival Greenbelt began in 1974 with 2,000 people but hosted over 20,000 in August 2005.[1] The inaugural Spring Harvest of 1979 involved 2,700 people whereas over 60,000 attended in April 2005. Spring Harvest, New Wine and even Keswick have all evolved beyond the event themselves and are effectively brands fostering particular Christian sub-cultures with diversified operations in holidays, resources, publishing and merchandizing. It really is possible to have 'been there,

Many Christians returning from festival struggle to assimilate their festival experiences within local church life

seen that, bought the t-shirt' and probably the CD, wristband and car-sticker as well!

Growing up in a small church with few young people, my first encounter with Spring Harvest produced a mind-blowing sense of being part of something 'bigger' and something 'real.' Worshipping with over five hundred other teenagers who were excited about their faith and expecting to encounter God remains a major milestone in my Christian journey. And just as I have enjoyed the faith-building dynamic of festival, so equally I have suffered the withdrawal symptoms that follow in the face of return to the mundane earthiness of 'normal life.' Many Christians returning from festival struggle to assimilate their festival experiences within local church life and attempts to integrate the two can have a destabilizing influence on the home community. It is often possible to trace the inverse relationship between dissipating enthusiasm and increased frustration as it slowly dawns that, like real ale, festival does not travel very well!

Furthermore, in recent years I have been awakened afresh to an entirely different form of festival, namely those particular days in the church calendar 'celebrating' significant events in the life of Christ and important saints. Quite often the sole distinctive of these 'liturgical festivals' is the insertion of specifically appointed set prayers at a few points in the liturgy. As I have wrestled with the wider significance of festivals in our church life, there have been two achingly obvious responses to my perennial pondering as to why we feel we have to go away to festivals to enjoy holy revelry. First, the 'going away,' stepping beyond the home context, must be significant to the experience itself. Second, maybe the church has forgotten how to party at home!

Beginning with these rudimentary observations this booklet will explore the role of corporate celebration and feasting within the life of the contemporary church. I sketch a theological model of festival which draws on the depictions of ancient Israelite worship presented in the Old Testament. I then offer this model as a tool for evaluating the celebratory character of our worship. More of a reconnaissance mission than a full-blown expedition, my aim is to stimulate church leaders and congregations to re-examine, and if necessary reclaim, the festive dimension of worship both within their local community and through participating in the wider 'festival scene.'

My prayer is that ancient wineskins might still provide clues as to how we can increase our enjoyment of new wine in our generation.

Festival Time

2

The dusty tomes of the Pentateuch may seem an unlikely place to start looking for a Christian theology of festival.

But since we have been grafted in 'to share the rich root of the olive tree' (Rom 11.17), we have much to gain from discerning the wisdom and value in our precious inheritance. Psalm 119 reveals how Israel regarded Torah (or Law) as a gift of grace, nurturing the covenant relationship which bound them together with God—they would be his people and he would be their God (Ex 6.7–8). God would be with Israel to accomplish his purposes, blessing them richly and the whole world through them. This relationship was thus the foundation of Israel's existence, identity, purpose (Gen 12.2–3) and hence her worship.

The books of the Pentateuch (Genesis to Deuteronomy) emphasize different facets of worship. In the so-called Book of the Covenant (Ex 20–23) the focuses of Deuteronomy (on covenantal obedience) and of Leviticus (on ritual holiness) are melded together to express the worship required of 'royal priests and a holy nation' (Ex 19.6). 'What is required in worship is not sacrifice but obedience…Obedience is the requisite for true worship, but not a substitute, for the rituals declare who the people are in relation to God.'[2]

Though looked on with suspicion by some, ritual is simply the commonly understood and anticipated modes of expression and behaviour by which a community seeks to engage with God. 'Every community of faith develops rites and customs functionally comparable to those priestly/congregational regulations from the 5th and 6th centuries BCE.'[3] This is true even of charismatic and pentecostal worship.[4]

Question for reflection

Have you explored how our Jewish roots might inform and enrich Christian spirituality and worship?

Example

One North-West church has found that regularly celebrating the festivals of Passover and Tabernacles has made a significant contribution towards building a sense of church community. Eating, dancing, laughing and worshipping together has enabled people not just to learn about, but also experience the significance of many of the Old Testament symbols such as light, water, bread, branches and so on. These are foundational to a fuller appreciation of Jesus' own words and actions and indeed the Christian hope expressed in the Epistles and Revelation.

The Structure of Sabbath Time

Life in ancient Israel was shaped by the relationship between festival and non-festival time and structured by the underlying principle of Sabbath observance (Lev 23.3). In keeping the Sabbath, Israel imitated God's rhythm of working to create and sustain, then stopping to enjoy the 'very-goodness' of creation.

Our concept of holiness is all too often dominated by perceptions of essential purity (on being set apart *from*) when it may have more to do with participating, delighting and existing in glorious wholeness and perfection (being set apart *for*). The Sabbath rhythm enabled Israel to revel with God in creation's goodness thereby becoming 'holy, as he is holy' (Lev 19.2). In contrast to contemporary society in which rest is either a bonus enjoyed when work is sufficiently complete or enforced by exhaustion, God requires us not to work *until* the Sabbath but to rest *on* the Sabbath. Work serves rest: 'holy days are not leftovers…they are the core that gives definition and purpose to everything else.'[5]

Questions for Reflection

How does our corporate worship release us to play with God in the goodness of creation? How might our worship incorporate such a dimension?

Two Modern Examples of Sabbath Festival

One West Midlands church experimented with a 'New Sunday Experience,' a Sunday morning given over to a short all-age worship service followed by a host of recreational opportunities from cycling to watercolour painting. This celebration of divine and human creativity culminated in a shared meal.

Another cell-based congregation draws its eclectic congregation together for a family Sunday once a month—a full day's programme of worshipping, eating, creating, exercising and playing together. The cells meet mid-week leaving other Sunday's free for more informal fellowship or family time.

The Highlights of Festival Time

If Sabbath provided life with rhythm and structure, it was the three annual pilgrimage feasts that were undoubtedly the highlights of the nation's worshipping life. Psalm 122 expresses the eager anticipation of pilgrims setting off to Jerusalem for the festival.

The **Feast of Unleavened Bread** and **Passover** may well take their timing from Canaanite ceremonies marking the start of the barley harvest, and the moving of flocks to new pasture. Whatever their 'original' meaning, the Israelites historicized them both in relation to the Exodus and combined them into a re-enactment of the first Passover meal and hasty flight from Egypt. Each festival the people shared in the Exodus experience and so this community 'memory' of origin and identity was passed from generation to generation.[6]

The **Festival of Weeks** marked the end of the grain harvest—seven weeks after the first sheaf was offered to God. The prescribed ritual involves journeying 'from wherever you live' (Lev 23.17) to a central sanctuary and bringing thanksgiving offerings 'in proportion to the blessings the Lord your God has given you' (Deut 16.10). The entire community, priests, slaves, stranger, widow and orphan,were invited to feast and share in God's plenteous provision. Later the festival became associated with the giving of the Sinai covenant.

The **Festival of Tabernacles** (or **Booths**) was the most esteemed and crowded of the pilgrimage feasts. At the close of the agricultural year farmers could afford to rejoice exuberantly with friends and family for seven full days. The scale of the celebrations are emphasized by the sacrifices prescribed for each day of the feast, far exceeding those required of other festivals (Num 29.12–38). The booths were the temporary shelters in which the people dwelt during the feast. These became associated with God's protection and provision for the people during their desert wanderings after the Exodus.

Roots and History

The agricultural roots of the festivals are clear; however, they were each historicized in order to link them to God's mighty acts in salvation history. Israel thanked her Creator but also remembered her Redeemer. Over time the form and meaning of the celebrations gradually evolved as the community reflected on their significance in particular historical contexts (see for example 2 Chr 35.18 and Neh 8). The festivals came to serve as milestones on a continuing journey, serving to build, sustain and transfer the story of the God who acted in the past to save his people, who provides for their present needs and who has a glorious destiny for them to fulfil. The festivals were more than mere celebrations of communal identity, by immersing people in this historical narrative they continually re-constituted that which they celebrated.

Contemporary festival events function in a similar way to these ancient celebrations, often booked up months in advance they are the eagerly awaited highlight of many Christians' year. They punctuate our Christian journey like waymarkers by which we can retrace our journey of faith. Spring Harvest have recognized this continuity in that their themes for 2006/7/8 are intended to interlink, enabling a story to unfold and develop from year to year.

The Jewish festivals were more than an annual event; they formed a liturgical calendar that shaped the worshipping life of the people throughout the entire year. For Israel the festival represented God's presence at the conjunction of sacred time, sacred space and sanctified community. But do Christians really need special festival time? Is not God, like Coca Cola, available anytime, anyplace, anywhere? Is not every Sunday Easter Sunday?

Part of me agrees, and yet, like Syndrome, the villain in Disney's *The Incredibles,* I wonder whether 'if everything is special, then nothing is special.' I have increasingly come to value the framework of the liturgical calendar and Christian seasons. They provide a disciplined space in which to explore God's story with the world and to discover and understand my place within that unfolding narrative. My appreciation of the hope and joy of Christmas, for example, has been deepened through sharing in the waiting of Advent as we wrestle with divine promise in the face of human reality. Epiphany forces me to ask tough questions about who this child is, why he came and how I allow him to shape my life and have an impact on the world through me.

Questions for Reflection

1 What gives shape and structure to worship in your community? When are the highlights in the worshipping life of your church?

2 When are the highlights? How do they differ from 'ordinary' worship? Would you describe any of them as joyous and celebratory feasts?

3 Rowan Williams recently encouraged efforts towards identifying fresh commemorations or injecting existing ones with dimensions of recent global and/or local significance. How does the pattern of worship enable your local church to recognise and celebrate its own story within the overarching story of God's action throughout history? How, for example, might you incorporate the particular challenges and opportunities facing your community this Spring into your worship during Lent?

Festival Place

3

Place and Presence

The Jewish festivals were to be celebrated 'before the Lord' (Ex 23.17) and were probably associated with regional sanctuaries before Israel's worship was focussed in Jerusalem. Whilst the Lord was understood to be present at the festivals to receive the people's worship it is overly simplistic to assume that he was thus said to be limited to this location. Prophetic ministry and exilic experience bore witness that God was not temporally or spatially constrained, but freely chose to meet his people in the particularity of festival time and festival place. The Temple was graciously provided and furnished by God with symbolic and ritual stimuli not as the sole, but perhaps the supreme, opportunity for Israel to perceive his presence.[7] Bound as we are to the material sphere, humanity can apprehend the universal only through the particularity of God's self-revelatory initiative in time and place—the 'rents in the opacity of history where God's concrete engagement to change the world becomes visible.'[8] The vivid memories (Ps 63.2) and eager anticipation (Ps 84) of such glimpses revealed in the Psalms express the privilege of participating in festival worship, a key identity marker of any true Israelite.

Divine encounter is ultimately located not in place but in the person of Jesus Christ made present by the Spirit

For the Christian, divine encounter is ultimately located not in place but in the person of Jesus Christ made present by the Spirit. Jerome asserted that 'access to the court of heaven is as easy from Britain as it is from Jerusalem.' However, as physical beings we are affected by places; they become familiar to us, we assign them characteristics and associate feelings with them such as fear, comfort, despair and excitement. Thus we relate to places as well as in them, and furthermore this response to place affects our interactions in that place. Celtic theology contains the notion of the 'thin place,' a physical space in which human awareness of God's presence seems to be increased. Place can affect our interaction with God, playing an active role in evoking and shaping the divine-human encounter. However, I demur at the notion that such participation endows place with an enduring inherent sacred quality. Whilst Butlins, Minehead has been holy ground in my Christian experience, I doubt whether it would be so in quite the same way if I revisited in a non-Spring Harvest week!

Place and Event

There is a close relationship between place and event. Is my awe at the Tower of London caused by my response to the physical space, my awareness of the things that have transpired there or a complex combination of both? Festivals are events; however, they are events which both occur in, and are shaped by, the places which stage them. Greenbelt recently moved from Castle Ashby in Northampton to Cheltenham and people familiar with both venues agree that this change has had a noticeable impact on the event. The topography and facilities of the new site have affected the nature of activities, the atmosphere and possibly even the diversity of attenders, contributing to an increasingly 'civilized' experience. If places shape events, then equally our experience of place is bound up with the events they have staged and, more significantly, the identity-shaping stories inspired by these events.[9] Such stories have great power, connecting those who share them together and also uniting and aligning them according to the predominant themes within the story.

Place and Pilgrimage

Pilgrimage is a near universal human phenomenon, an embodied quest typically directed towards places associated with divine-human encounter.[10] It combines temporal and spatial dimensions—the Jews travelled to feast before the Lord at the appointed times and in the appointed place. Pilgrimages are 'liminoid' events, times of transition between stable life stages or situations…

> … in which previous orderings of thought and behaviour are subject to revision and criticism, when hitherto unprecedented modes of ordering relations between ideas and people become possible and desirable.[11]

Pilgrimage affords people a period of release from the constricting structures of their regular routine into the freedom of anti-structure

The medieval era was the zenith for pilgrimage, which were often conducted as acts of penitence with the hope of gaining merit. However, we must recognize that for many people it also represented the only legitimate opportunity to escape a lifetime of local restriction imposed by the feudal system and community responsibilities. It was not therefore surprising that people usually preferred to travel to more distant places rather than visiting the local shrine. The increasing popularity of contemporary, secular and religious pilgrimages and festivals may be partly motivated by similar desires to escape the suffocating fiefdom of our consumer society. Pilgrimage affords people a period of release from the constricting structures of their regular routine into the freedom of anti-structure, to conceive and desire 'hitherto unprecedented modes of being'; time away and time out are equally significant ingredients of this creative process.

There are clear affinities between contemporary festival and pilgrimage. Both are motivated by a desire to encounter God on holy ground and involve stepping outside regular existence, and into a place invested with expectation, hope and anticipation of such experience. This investment of faith, time, money and perhaps other things can 'cleanse the doors of perception,' increasing our ability to hear and receive from the Spirit. Symbols that have been rendered almost invisible through over-familiarity within the home setting can, in the festival context, have fresh impact, regain their communicative power and be transformed into vehicles of sacramental encounter.[12]

In the same way that festival time exists by distinction from ordinary time, so a change in environment is a major dimension of festival. However, there is often an important balance between distinction from the home context and familiarity with the festival environment. The increased expectations and anticipation of enjoying God and one another are partly based upon the community's corporate memory of previous occasions. One church in the North-West returned regularly to a conference centre over a number of years effectively producing a 'thin place' in which it was as if they developed an instinct for engaging with the Spirit in that particular place. For other churches it might be the annual trip to New Wine or Spring Harvest. Times like this often have a natural season, but it can be difficult to leave these familiar places and routines behind in order to discern new places God is preparing to enjoy with us. The Israelites were first and foremost commanded to celebrate 'before the Lord'—it was not the place, but his presence in the place that was significant.

A recent advert directed towards non-church attenders read 'Do not go Far East to find yourself—you might be just around the corner'! Festival-goers may similarly need to be encouraged not to depend on far or thin places but equipped to seek God at home. Whereas festival is focused on place and event, pilgrimage emphasizes the journey—the process of getting from home to the 'holy place' and back again. There is explicit recognition that the fruits of pilgrimage should enrich the life of the community upon the pilgrim's re-integration at home. Prospective medieval pilgrims prepared spiritually and physically not just for their departure but also for their return to the community.

Records show how the Lincoln Guild directed each member to give a penny to the pilgrim on departure and to celebrate their return by going out to meet them and accompanying them to the church.[13]

The pilgrim performed, at least in part, a representative function, going on their behalf and returning for their benefit

This model—of the pilgrim and community anticipating and preparing for the difficulties of assimilating festival experiences upon returning home—is worth commending to contemporary churches. It is interesting that the members of the Lincoln Guild all invested in the pilgrim's journey, the community were thus formally involved in both their departure and their return. The pilgrim performed, at least in part, a representative function, going on their behalf and returning for their benefit. Churches today might be significantly enriched if those who remain at home could grasp a similar vision of partnership in the festival and its fruits.

Questions for reflection

- Do we have a 'far' place where we can cultivate our receptivity and consciousness of God's presence (both individually and corporately)?
- Is this still the place where God wants to meet with our community this year—or is the Holy Spirit leading us to new places?
- How does our celebration in the far place enrich our life together at home? How might we prepare to go and return from festival? Do we need to?

Festival Drama 4

Ritual

Every culture has rituals, the way people greet one another, celebrate marriages or conduct worship, for example. These rituals are the main way in which a culture expresses its understanding of the world, and the formal method it has of celebrating and communicating 'how things are.' Israel's festivals were composite rituals composed of various acts each expressing a part of Israel's basic understanding of God's work, taking them 'from bondage to Covenant liberty.' In many ways the biblical accounts are frustrating, providing details about times, places and priestly rubric but no comprehensive depiction of 'a pilgrim's experience of festival'! However, by interweaving fragments of narrative description and poetic details gleaned from Psalms a rich tapestry of festival experience can be inferred:

> There were acts of purification, dramas of God's victory over his enemies, recital of important aspects of the covenant, and sacrifices which expressed...praise and thanks, atonement and reconciliation. Worshippers were deeply involved physically, in washing, dancing, shouting, prostration, clapping, singing and feasting.[14]

It has been suggested that the covenant renewal rituals particularly associated with the Feast of Tabernacles (Deut 31.10–11; Neh 8) can be summarized by a threefold model—Remember, Read, Renew. As the people gathered together in God's presence to hear Torah they would be reminded of the covenant, of God's faithfulness in the face of their own waywardness, and be prompted to commit themselves to a renewed relationship. (The Worship, Word, Response model favoured within many contemporary churches performs a very similar ritual function). The danger in looking to uncover the 'original' function of ancient rituals is that we risk missing the point that ritual can be performed simply because it is enjoyable, in the same way that worship is sometimes described as a 'glorious waste of time.' Worship in the Western church can easily become sober and functional, but in Israel it did not. In order to encapsulate the nature of festival ritual we might supplement the above model with a fourth dimension, 'Rejoice.' The Festival was a single and holistic expression of worship—from the sober awe of the sacrificial offerings to the exuberant, excessive feasting and drinking.[15] God both demanded and provided for joyous worship that was not restricted to spiritual piety or liturgical recitation, but embraced the whole being—body, mind and spirit were employed to celebrate the wonder of covenant life with God.

I am immediately challenged by the comprehensive nature of this worship experience which seeks to touch the spirit by engaging the body through colour, aroma, sound, flavour and physical movement, and the imagination with drama and symbol. A strength of contemporary festival events is that their scale and resources can help them identify Christians whose particular giftings can offer a similar breadth and richness to worship. The menu for celebrating liturgical festivals is often rather narrow in comparison. This must have an impact on people's ability to connect with worship since different personality groups respond to different stimuli. Clearly such a comprehensive feast has resource implications but this may well provide the opportunity for occasional collaborative celebrations in which local churches can pool and draw upon their respective talents and traditions.

Ritual as Sacred Drama

Whilst the function of ritual is hotly debated it is most commonly conceived as a communication medium, conveying underlying meaning through employing static signs and more dynamic symbolic action. It is not simply declarative but involves demonstrating and participating in that which it expresses. At the festival you could see and taste, as opposed to merely hearing, the truth of God's goodness.

Rituals enable us to experience religious truth at physical, sensual, emotional and spiritual levels

This transformative power of ritual is increasingly being recognized. As humans we have the capacity to evoke alternative realities, able to live in both the world 'as is' and the world 'as if.' The Torah took shape whilst Israel was a Persian colony and yet its vision of worship asserted that Yahweh was in control and Israel his elected people. The return from exile would later confirm this vision but it was hardly supported by the evidence available at the time in Babylon. Rituals thus enact a worldview which extends 'beyond the realities of everyday life to wider ones which correct and complete them'[17] and thereby expose the 'real' as a mere shadow of the 'really, real.' They are not merely escapism, or utopian dreaming but enable us to experience religious truth both consciously and subconsciously at physical, sensual, emotional and spiritual levels. This experience of truth can both challenge and consolidate our self-understanding. Thus whilst ritual expresses identity, our participation in ritual actually re-constitutes identity.

New Wine 2006 is entitled 'Heavenbound' and invites people to 'take time out to enjoy a small taste of heaven.' Just as for Babylonian exiles, God-given glimpses of his eternal kingdom radically reorientate our present perspectives, increasing our hunger to draw others in 'to discover all that God has for us here and now on our way to that final destination.'

Contemporary Festival Ritual

There is great diversity across the spectrum of contemporary Christian festivals. However, the vast majority will include specific acts of worship, ministry, teaching, fellowship and recreation, emphasized to varying degrees. Thus Creation Fest, whilst predominantly a music festival, also aims to spread the gospel, establish Christians in the basics of Christianity, proclaim the authority of Scripture and bring churches together in unity. The Keswick convention offers 'a holiday with a purpose,' highlighting 'careful exposition of Scripture' and also anticipating uplifting worship. The festivals seek to resource the wider church, equipping them for growth and action in their local community.

According to the definition of ritual as relatively formalized, repeated, corporate, value-oriented and goal-seeking activities these festivals are clearly themselves ritual activities. Festival-goers learn how to participate in the rituals of the particular festival including how demonstratively to engage in worship, how to make a personal response to God, the particular jargon to employ, even where to locate the car sticker! As with pilgrimage, people leave role and status behind, expressing themselves with greater freedom and displaying greater openness to God and one another than in their home contexts. Ritual facilitates this risk-taking by providing the safety of a familiar routine alongside an edge of anticipation and expectation of God's presence.

Festival joyously celebrates the privilege of being in covenant relationship with our God. Festival rituals reinforce the story of our faith and help us see beyond the reality of our situations to glimpse God's reality, the kingdom which is 'a long way off, but inside it there are quite different things going on' (Dylan Thomas). Research amongst devotees of the Catholic saint Padre Pio in Italy revealed the danger of conceiving the 'real' and the 'really, real' as parallel realities. Many of these followers effectively withdrew from the local community in an attempt to spend as much time as possible in close proximity to the shrine, apparently attempting to set up permanent residence in ritual time and space.[18] Whilst this is an extreme example, there is often a temptation to replicate the festival experience within the home context, as if festival could supersede

Festival rituals reinforce the story of our faith and help us see beyond the reality of our situations to glimpse God's reality

ordinary time. This is further evidence of the failure to understand the proper relationship between these modes of Christian community.

In closing a recent Christian conference the host suggested that the sense of God's presence experienced by many delegates had not been unusual but just 'ordinary church.' I disagreed with him initially. However, I am beginning to see what he meant. St Francis received the vision that radically reoriented his life at the Portiuncula, an abandoned Chapel in the Umbrian countryside, to which he returned frequently. It has been suggested that the inspiration he received there enabled him to regularly discern wonder everywhere in what others viewed with scorn.[19] Similarly, festival celebration affords us a glimpse of God's vision for the world and energizes us to work to reveal what is already there, waiting to be uncovered within our home contexts. It is not festival that we uncover but the truths affirmed, celebrated and tasted at the festival, namely the reality of God's reign and rule. It can be hard to spot the wheat for the weeds, but at harvest the kingdom will be fully revealed and the final celebrations begin (see Matt 13.24–30).

Question for reflection

How does our festival experience equip us to perceive the reality of God's kingdom during ordinary time?

The ancient Jewish festivals recognized that they depended upon both God's grace and the labours of the people between festivals. It was the fruit of ordinary time that furnished the feast. There is a sense in which those responsible for organizing current festival, whether at the large events or at local liturgical celebrations, have a duty to ensure that the festival similarly 'honours' ordinary time. Firstly, there should be an appropriate awareness of the risk of fostering dependency upon festival experience through countering unhelpful emphases on personalities and scale of performance. Secondly, the reality and value of our everyday experience needs to be acknowledged and affirmed within the celebratory rites so that festival does not ignore or offer escape from the ordinary but helps us see through it and beyond it.

Contemporary Christmas places an unbearable strain upon finances and relationships in many households—how might our celebrations enable our community to acknowledge, transcend and transform that reality?

5 Festival Community

Communitas—the Festival 'Feeling'

In the introduction I described my teenage experience of Spring Harvest in terms of a sense of 'being part' of something 'real,' of sensing an energy of expectancy and anticipation of encountering God. These are symptoms of communitas, 'moments in and out of time' when the normative structures, statuses and roles in life are temporarily suspended and give rise to an intense experience of spontaneous all-embracing community.[20] The businessmen's dinner I attended at the Café Royal in London to watch England's World Cup victory over Argentina in 2002 produced somewhat similar phenomena!

There is a close link between ritual and communitas. In enacting the stories at the heart of a culture, ritual focuses upon and quickens the bonds of communion that define a community's shared sense of identity. This experience of communitas then stimulates further ritual activity as those involved recognize how the drama can help bring the community to life. Communitas offers a moment of revelation, a moment of critique and a moment of equipping. The deep sense of open relatedness and mutual understanding offers a glimpse of how things could and should be, interpreted by Christians as a taste of God's intention for humanity and a foretaste of the kingdom. This nectar of possibility contrasts with the acid reality of much of human society and can provoke a search to identify the source of the 'souring' influences. Finally, the sense of unity and common vision entailed in communitas offers a revitalizing power, equipping people to act as transformative agents within the structures to which they return.

As with anything that feels good there is a temptation to 'capture' and systematize communitas, treating it as goal to be achieved rather than an integral phase within the continuing process of human social life. This raises important issues for those organizing and attending festivals. Firstly, there is the natural tendency to focus on how to produce the best possible festival experience. Communitas, however, cannot be produced for consumption but is a fruit of sharing in mutual, vulnerable and open relationships. The second danger also stems from our obsession with experience. Like joy, communitas is not an abstract quality of the individual. As we have joy in something so communitas arises out of shared identity, purpose and meaning. Unless our festival is rooted in celebrating God's past (and anticipating his future) action in the world and especially in the life of the particular faith community, then it will soon become vacuous and unsatisfying. During the Live8 concert in July 2005 the BBC's political editor Andrew Marr commented that people are willing to join in a moment but not a movement. For the Christian, moments of festival are inextricably linked to, and spring from, our sharing in the missionary movement of the church.

Inclusive Festivity?

Psalm 133 describes the communitas enjoyed by the Israelites gathered in Jerusalem for the Festivals. In holy time and space these pilgrims are united as one family and invited to dine together in the presence of the Lord. This wonderful privilege is compared to being anointed with richly perfumed oil, a custom reserved for honoured guests. One commentator suggests that the dew of Hermon does not fall on Zion (v 3) but 'runs down to the "parched" hill country.'[21] Might this portray the blessing of God flowing from festival and extending year-round to the entire nation? In reaching the 'parched grounds' it ensures that no-one is excluded from sharing in the feast.

Everyone was expected to attend the feast, not just freemen and their families but servants and slaves, widows, orphans and strangers (Deut 16.11). Nehemiah specifically reminded the exiles that 'choice food and sweet drinks' should be sent to those who had nothing before the celebration of Tabernacles could begin (Neh 8.10). The proclamation that the Lord has redeemed his enslaved people and provided them with an abundant land was made tangible; everyone was invited to, quite literally, taste the truth!

This radically inclusive dimension offers perhaps the biggest challenge to our contemporary festivals. The Message 2000 project in Manchester represented a different model for festival which has subsequently been replicated around the country in London (Soul in the City 2004), Liverpool (Merseyfest 2005) and Belfast (Summer Madness). These events aim to proclaim and demonstrate the kingdom of God within the heart of urban life, by partnering in locally conceived social action projects and staging communal celebrations. Merseyfest released 8,000 people to work on the community projects during the week and then staged a free weekend event attended by over 30,000 people daily and featuring music, dance, a skatepark, urban arts, an interactive family zone and much more. And these were no 'hit and run' events. The vision for the Manchester festivals of 2000 and 2003 developed within the Message Trust's existing commitment and involvement across the city. The success of the initiative depended upon the networks of local churches and effective partnerships with community bodies and authorities built up over several years. The festivals provide profile and give an impetus to the ongoing mission but it is the sustained presence and long-term commitment to local communities that engenders the trust and respect which wins a hearing for the gospel.

Which Community?

Old Testament festivals involved the entire nation and the reason for this is quite clear. These occasions were the means of maintaining the nation's unity, binding tribes and clans together as they remembered and re-enacted their founding narratives. In this way their common identity as God's chosen people was not merely celebrated but continuously renewed. With contemporary festivals it is very unlikely that an entire church could attend even if every member were so inclined. Home congregations comprise various and sometimes overlapping groups 'aligned' with various festivals or none.

Common identity does not require identical clones and indeed such groups can provide access to a wide spectrum of resources and allow for greater awareness and openness to the breadth of Christian tradition and experience. However, the question arises as to whose narrative is being told. What is the identity that is being affirmed and established? Festival 'structures' are developing into brands and even sub-cultures in which leadership teams can attract celebrity status as personally holding the key to releasing festival experience. Each festival community develops its own narrative and identity, which need to make sense and be critiqued within the context of the local church community to which people belong. This is where prior preparation for the return from festival may help, committing us to openly discuss and discern how this year's festival might continue to enrich us personally and also our community. Such a process might prevent a credibility gap developing between festival and local identity and discourage people rejecting one in favour of the other.

Jewish festivals were 'pure acts of alternative community'[22] in which the people acknowledged and celebrated their common identity. Covenant life with God was reinvigorated as the people came bearing choice offerings, to declare their gratitude and reliance on God's provision. Covenant life with one another was renewed as the marginalized were included in the feast, the harvest gleanings left for the poor, and national unity constituted as all twelve tribes gathered as a united body.

Questions for Reflection

1 How does the worshipping life of your church openly demonstrate, and invite people to taste, the goodness of God?

2 How do corporate celebrations contribute to building unity in your local church?

6 Theological Reflection

Christian Joy

Whatever Happened to Joy?

I have often wondered whether the church should face charges for advertising Communion services as 'celebrations' when so often they more closely reflect 'commiserations.' As early as the 4th Century John Chrysostom recognized that for many Christians the liturgy appeared unattractive and tedious compared with its Jewish counterpart. Indeed, in the light of an instinct to spiritualize religious experience the earthy nature of Jewish festivity can appear almost sacrilegious. Duffy's depiction of life in mediaeval Britain portrays an integration between 'a piety…rooted in stillness and looking …and a piety which seems geared to movement and elaborate communal celebration.'[23] The holy days of the liturgical calendar, which marked the passing of time, were both sacred and social highlights uniting the community in faith and festivity. The Reformers viewed them less positively, holding them responsible for reducing productivity and encouraging laziness, debauchery and social unrest. It was not long before the baby of joyous social feasts joined its siblings of religious imagery, music and drama, in being expelled with the bathwater of religious exploitation, indulgences, superstition and licentious excess. Even Christmas was abolished du,ring the Puritan austerity of Cromwell's Commonwealth (1649–1660), as a result of which it is still technically illegal to eat Mince Pies on Christmas Day!

Whilst many factors have contributed to the demise of joy perhaps the biggest single influence has been the loss of confidence provoked over the last century by the horrific state of the world, human atrocity and widespread suffering. Such misery can cause us to question the appropriateness of expressing joy, leading to guilt due to the feeling that we should, and perhaps could, be more purposefully occupied.

Such misery can cause us to question the appropriateness of expressing joy

Vocation to Joy

Christians often appear to perceive 'Christian joy' as not merely distinct from, but potentially even tainted by, the joy of natural human experience: 'very often these days we have joy without God, or God without joy.'[24] This diminished experience of joy can be traced back to a neo-Platonic elevation of the 'permanent' transcendent over the 'transitory' material. Authentic joy, however, refuses to remain caged in the soul, but embraces us holistically, demanding to be expressed through our entire physical, emotional, mental as well as spiritual existence. If Genesis affords work and enjoyment equal status within the human vocation, the *Westminster Catechism* goes even further: 'Man's chief end is to glorify God and to enjoy him forever.' In his *Theology and Joy* Moltmann asserts that the meaning of human life does not exist in demonstrating utility and achievement but simply in joy—joy in our, and God's, existence. He suggests that creation shares our prioritization of existential joy over usefulness—even 'the birds are singing much more than Darwin permits'[25]—and also our frustration when this joy is denied (Rom 8.20–1). Celebratory joy involving re-living foundational narratives, with singing, dancing, feasting and praying, however, is both a uniquely human, and universal human, characteristic. To deny a corporeal dimension to holy joy is to deny both our humanity and God's gracious and abundant provision. It is also to deny the nature of Jesus' character and ministry.

Moltmann asserts that the meaning of human life does not exist in demonstrating utility and achievement but simply in joy

Jesus and Festival

The writer of John's gospel deliberately uses Jesus' presence at the Jewish feasts in order to present him sometimes as their fulfilment, sometimes as their re-interpretation, but never their negation. Jesus is portrayed as the true bread from heaven and the paschal Lamb (John 6.4, 13.1—Passover and Unleavened Bread), the water of life and light for the world (John 7.2—Tabernacles) and the embodiment of the tabernacling presence of God (John 10.22—Hanukah).[26] Jesus' festivity was not confined to institutional religion but spilled over into the whole of his life. The first miraculous sign at Cana involved supplying premier quality wine to prolong the, already well-lubricated, wedding celebrations—a resounding affirmation of corporeal as well as corporate celebration! The most natural reading of the Greek text of Matthew 9.18 suggests that the tax collectors and 'sinners' were eating in Jesus' house rather than Matthew's, when John's disciples questioned the appropriateness of his feasting and the Pharisees disapproved of his scandalously inclusive table fellowship. For Jesus the feast was a sign of the kingdom implying an abundance to be broken and shared, such that celebration was impossible unless the poor, needy, publicans and sinners could also participate.[27] This was radical openness with a core challenge. The sinners heard that they required a doctor (Matt 9.12) and were confronted, like Zacchaeus (Luke 19.8), with the need for costly repentance.

Joy flourishes in an environment of honesty and openness

This challenge did not destroy the festivity because Jesus was not afraid of openly revealing himself. Joy flourishes in an environment of honesty and openness whereas the fear of intimacy, hiding agendas and masking true identity can render the feast a disappointing sham.

Jesus' festive joy led him beyond the boundaries of social convention to the margins of humanity and opened him to share their suffering (Heb 12.2). I expect joy to be the opposite of suffering and yet paradoxically the deeper our fellowship in Christ's joy, the deeper our openness to embrace the world's suffering: 'Only those who are capable of joy can feel pain at their own and other people's suffering...Where freedom is near, the chains begin to hurt.'[28] Christian joy is neither masochistically identified with suffering nor restricted to a future hope once earthly pain has ended. Kingdom joy is real joy available now in a suffering world and one day to be made full in the presence of the returning King.

Paul and Festival

The final point to mention is Paul's apparent dismissal of the significance of 'special' days (Rom 14.5, Gal 4.10). In the context of tension between Gentiles and Jewish Christians in Rome, Paul exhorted the 'strong' who considered each day equally significant not to condemn those who continued to observe special days. Galatians reveals Paul's incredulity that Gentiles had been persuaded to adopt the sacred Jewish calendar. In each letter Paul contends for Christian freedom, recognizing that ardent legalists and zealous libertarians can be equally oppressive. Paul is not excluding the principle of Christian festival but refuting their necessity for salvation. We noted earlier how the festivals developed over time but always functioned to constitute, maintain and preserve Jewish identity for future generations. The New Testament was written in a different context, in expectation of an imminent *parousia*, and was not especially concerned to provide a blueprint for building and sustaining Christian identity and community for over two thousand years.

Questions for Reflection

1 'Joy is a command. Joylessness is a serious sin...It may be the sin most readily tolerated by the church.' Do you agree with John Ortberg's comments from his book *The Life You've Always Wanted*?

2 How do you cultivate joyfulness as a distinguishing characteristic of your church? Does God still encourage and enjoy hosting exuberant and excessive celebrations for his people (Deut 14:25-7)?

7 Re-appropriating Festival

Festival Summary

To review the argument so far I suggest that festival is:

- **Constituted** in the present by a propelling memory. The community's sense of identity and purpose are reinforced through remembering God's faithfulness in the past and anticipating the fulfilment of his promises for their future.
- **Consecrated** space and time to meet with God. Particular times and places are set aside and endowed with expectation and anticipation of engaging with the Spirit of God.
- **Celebratory** and revelatory ritual. People participate in joyful and excessive feasting, whereby the 'super-reality' of God's gracious and glorious rule is glimpsed beyond the mere reality of everyday existence.
- **Commitment** to renewing community life. The experience of joyful communitas stimulates the desire for deeper commitment to God and neighbour.
- **Central** to local church life—never reduced to a sideshow.
- **Characterized** by radical openness—taking the feast beyond the church perimeter.

Festival in the Local Church

Until recently I perceived festival as a super-celebration, an optional fourth level to the 'cell-congregation-celebration' model of church. However, festival is broader and more integral to our experience than that, a celebratory dimension of faith through which Christian identity is built and Christian community continually reinvigorated. I am not suggesting that we all rigorously adopt the liturgical calendar. However, we can all examine the shape and variety of our worship throughout the year in the light of the dimensions of festival we have identified.

What are the highlights of our life together and what makes these occasions distinctive? How do we enable our churches to spend time enjoying each other, having fun, eating together—simply to celebrate being the people of God? To what extent can the local community share in our celebrations?

The challenge of festival must be more than a gospel flavoured homily—it must demonstrate alternative ways of living

It may well be that to reclaim festival we have to challenge our own jaded misconceptions, liberate it from unhelpful cultural accretions and then re-imagine it for a new generation. The important question is 'What could this festival mean for this community at this time?' Take Christmas as an obvious example—last Christmas the nativity play and Christingle service each drew three times the typical congregation to the picturesque village church I attended. Initially positive about this 'mission opportunity,' I began to wonder whether we were in danger of providing a nostalgic entertainment service. The privatized family reunion and consumer carnage that is contemporary Christmas has apparently little to do with exploring the meaning of incarnation, affirming our common humanity and demonstrating God's goodwill toward humanity. The challenge of festival must be more than a gospel flavoured homily—it must demonstrate alternative ways of living. In 1972 a Texan prayer group asked themselves what Christmas might mean for them. The answer led them to take Christmas to people living on a Mexican waste dump and to the subsequent establishment of an ongoing humanitarian and evangelistic ministry.[29]

Could a harvest celebration for an urban community in 2006 take the form of a celebration of local life and productivity? Various community organizations such as schools, residents' associations, local businesses, retailers and so forth could be invited to participate in an exhibition and a service of thanksgiving before sharing a festive meal and entertainment. If you do not like the idea that is fine—but what might be relevant for your community?

Are there opportunities to recognize and celebrate the significance of belonging to the wider church in your area or region? Town–wide ecumenical celebrations can be both an important sign of Christian unity and actually deepen that unity by identifying common concerns, enabling networking, cooperation in ministry and sharing of resources. Such events reflect the origins of Mothering Sunday when people converged from local congregations to the 'mother' church of an area.

Festival Events and the Local Church

Many Christians, myself included, can testify to the fact that festival events have played a significant part as a vital catalyst and sustaining force for celebrating their faith and deepening their understanding of themselves and God. Festivals are extremely effective at opening the individual to a much larger world and the realization that they belong to this wider Christian community. If there is a potential weakness it lies in the relationship between the festival and the local church. Of course the festivals seek to equip, resource and envision local churches which they do by resourcing, equipping and envisioning thousands of individual Christians. Many of these people may well be frustrated in their attempts to share all they feel they have received within their home communities—even in churches which would in theory support their initiatives if they had time to think about it! The onus is I believe upon the local church to 'own' the festival, to acknowledge its occurrence and take time to address the question 'What might this festival event mean for our community this year?'

The onus is I believe upon the local church to 'own' the festival

The first thing the local church can do is go to festival! Perhaps more importantly they can go to festival together. The vicar of one Hertfordshire church asked his congregation to seriously consider choosing one festival and attending *en masse* or at least sending only two large groups to two different festivals. He believed the impact on church life would be significantly increased if the community shared and reflected together upon the same festival experience.

One thing we can certainly do is prepare in advance to go and return from festival. I am challenged by the fact that the Jews offered back to God the firstfruits of the harvest—they celebrated the fruit of their partnership with him in the harvest. Perhaps we might in the same way consider what we are bringing to the celebration; how have we seen God at work in our fields over the past year? What fruit do we have to thank him for? Festivals aim to resource the church so we need to be ready to exploit the opportunity they provide! They present themselves as quite natural milestones in the journey of the church, a time to pause and reflect on time past and be refreshed and equipped for the coming year. It might make sense to plan formal sessions back in the home context for feeding back and reviewing the festival and to adjust church planning and review processes to take on board fresh vision that might emerge.

In all this we must not forget that many people in our churches will not take part in festival events, and integrating the expectations, hopes and perhaps fears of those who went and those who stayed can be difficult but should not be ignored. Stereotypical contentious issues include the rapid overhaul of the worship playlist with the latest tunes from festival that have been so significant to those who went but do not have the same resonances for those who stayed. This situation raises two important issues. Firstly, the importance of clear communication to manage the expectations of the whole church with regard to why we go to festival, what we hope to receive and how the whole church can be enriched. Encouraging church members to share their stories of encountering God with the home church can be really beneficial but we might also want to consider that the Spirit may have been active at home too! Secondly, the festive dimension of local church life must not be neglected since for many people it is their only opportunity to experience the party.

The festive dimension of local church life must not be neglected

Last Word

Mike Yaconelli's memory of a Greenbelt Holy Communion reveals the transformative potential of festival for both ancient Jew and contemporary Christian:

> I was moved to tears just looking over the crowd and seeing black, white, old, young, punker, straight, children, elderly, worshipping God in total unity. For ninety minutes the real world of hatred, prejudice, pettiness and selfishness were forgotten. We were the invisible church made visible for an instant, and it was truly overwhelming. For a few fleeting moments I got a glimpse of what heaven will be like and I will never forget it.

Just as for the apostles on the mount of transfiguration, festival offers glimpses of glory not as an escape from real life but as a revelation of the 'really, real,' empowering us to discover the wonder of the kingdom amidst the ordinariness that awaits us at the foot of the mountain.

A bibliography is available on the Grove Books web site
www.grovebooks.co.uk

Notes

1 'Youth festival, music festival, political festival, evangelical festival, development festival, broke festival, harvest festival…there's something in all these myths about Greenbelt that is accurate, but nothing entirely true.' http://www.greenbelt.org.uk/aboutus

2 Ryken *et al*, *Dictionary of Biblical Imagery*, p 972.

3 See D E Albrecht, *Rites in the Spirit; A Ritual Approach to Pentecostal/Charismatic Spirituality* (Sheffield: Sheffield Academic Press, 1999).

4 S E Balentine, *Leviticus* (IBC) (Louisville: John Knox Press, 2000) p 7 (parentheses mine).

5 *ibid*, p 181.

6 See W Brueggemann, *Deuteronomy* (AOTC) (Nashville: Abingdon Press, 2001) p 174.

7 Cohn, cited by S E Balentine, *The Torah's Vision of Worship* (Minneapolis: Fortress Press, 1999) p 192.

8 T Gorringe, cited by J Inge, *A Christian Theology of Place* (Aldershot, Hampshire: Ashgate, 2003) p 67.

9 See also Inge, p 84. I am indebted to Inge for his clear and persuasive arguments concerning the role of place in divine-human encounter and in the shaping of religious identity.

10 See J G Davies, *Pilgrimage Yesterday and Today: Why? Where? How?* (London: SCM, 1988) for an introductory exploration of Christian pilgrimage.

11 V Turner and E Turner, *Image and Pilgrimage in Christian Culture* (Oxford: Basil Blackwell, 1978) p 2.

12 *ibid*, p 11.

13 See D Dyas, 'Mediaeval Patterns of Pilgrimage—A Mirror for Today?' in C Bartholomew and F Hughes (eds), *Explorations in a Christian Theology of Pilgrimage* (Aldershot, Hampshire: Ashgate, 2004).

14 D W Hardy and D F Ford, *Praising and Knowing God* (Philadelphia: Westminster Press, 1985) p 39.

15 See 1 Sam 1.14–15 where Eli assumes Hannah is drunk—probably on the occasion of this feast! Nehemiah commanding the people to respond to the reading

of the Law not with weeping but to celebrate by feasting on the best food and drink available (Neh 8.10).

16 The opposite case can be argued for most festival events—their strength lies in their marginal position with respect to particular denominational structures, from where they can offer both challenge and encouragement.

17 Geertz, cited in Balentine's, *The Torah's Vision of Worship*, p 62.

18 McKevitt's research is documented in J Eade, and M J Sallnow (eds), *Contesting the Sacred; The Anthropology of Christian Pilgrimage* (London: Routledge) pp 77–97.

19 See Lane, cited by Inge, p 77.

20 In this section I am indebted to Turner's discussion of communitas in V Turner, *The Ritual Process; Structure and Anti-Structure* (New York: Aldine de Gruyter, 1969).

21 H-J Kraus, *Psalms 60–150: A Commentary* (Minneapolis: Augsburg, 1989) p 484. Kraus' tradition-historical approach fails to engage with the significance of the Psalm for worship, but it is his translation that inspired my imagination!

22 See W Brueggemann, *Deuteronomy* (AOTC) (Nashville: Abingdon Press, 2001) p 177.

23 E Duffy, *The Stripping of the Altars; Traditional Religion in England 1400–1580* (New Haven: Yale University Press, 1992) p 38.

24 See the chapter on community and celebration in J Vanier, *Community and Growth* (Revised Edition) (London: DLT, 1979) pp 232–245, quotation taken from p 237.

25 J Moltmann, *Theology and Joy*, translated by R Ulrich (London: SCM Press, 1973) pp 42–3.

26 The pouring of water and all-night dancing by candle light were both Tabernacles ceremonies. Hanukah is an annual celebration of the reconsecration of Jerusalem's Temple during the inter-testamental period. *cf* S D B Moloney, SJ, (1998) *The Gospel of John* (Sacra Pagina) (Collegeville, Minnesota: The Liturgical Press, 1988) p 319.

27 See W Logister, 'A small theology of feasting' in P Post, G Rouwhorst, L van Tongeren, A Scheer (eds), *Christian Feast and Festival; The Dynamics of Western Liturgy and Culture* (Leuven: Peeters, 2001) pp 145–166.

28 J Moltmann, *Theology and Joy*, translated by R Ulrich (London: SCM Press, 1973) p 52.

29 R Laurentin, *Viva Christo Rey!* (Waco: Word, 1982) tells the story of God at work amongst the poor of El Paso Juarez on the border between Mexico and Texas.